Love
& Other Comforts
Poems for the Road

by
Christine Wren

First published in 2021 by Immortalise

contact: info@immortalise.com.au

© 2021 Christine Wren

The moral rights of the author have been asserted

All rights reserved. Except as permitted under the Australian Copyright Act 1968 (for example, a fair dealing for the purposes of study, research, criticism or review), no part of this book may be reproduced, stored in a retrieval system, communicated or transmitted in any form or by any means without prior written permission. All inquiries should be made to the author.

ISBN: 978-0-6450377-1-5

Cover design and typesetting by: Ben Morton

Cover image photo by Kelsey Curtis on Unsplash

Love
& Other Comforts

To be loved well, is to be loved in spite of your worst sin, lack or misdemeanour. Not overlooking it, but accepting it as part of the whole. i.e. … you.

Falling and failing are usually my best teachers. Our life journey is never a straight line, but a series of convoluted meanderings into beautiful moments, foxholes, minefields and perhaps, home.

So many paradoxes. In is out, up is down, but all can be well. Eventually.

What a relief to hang up the masks we hide behind, and dare to be simply: ourselves, unmasked.

I have been writing for a long while and find words an essential richness to any form of life.

I love it that God calls us his poems. I love it that we are tattooed on his hand.

So, fellow pilgrims, fallen and failing, heroes and villains, successes and failures-

I wish you a Buon Camino.

As you travel your own path , with your own faltering steps, may God's richest blessings astound and surround you.

Thanks for listening.

Foreword

This book is a collection of reality. As the title says it is about love. Human and Divine.

Chris's poems need to be read slowly and carefully, with no exceptions. They hold much wisdom from deep life experience and need to be handled carefully, to honour yourself and the writer. They are not about ideals or fluff or romance, they are about reality, uncertainty and healing.

Some images require a sitting with. The juxtapositions, the contrasts and the sounds can take a while to be seen heard and responded to. Like "Wind wafts a shiver through the tall grasses" (from *Iona*) And "… crimson gobs of sweet" (from *Wood Cottage, Suffolk*)

Taken as a whole, this collection tells us that love is complex, sometimes it works, but sometimes it's simply not enough. The poems come from deep and tender life experiences; like *Glass* and *Betrayal* and *No trespassing*. These are the poems of one who knows betrayal, disappointment, false starts, and then the final triumph that doesn't end with a crescendo but a gentle cup of tea.

Favourite one? *Kissed Alive Again*, which reminds us that love provides joy and hope, but fear and challenge. Summed up in the words "Pace myself, brace myself. And let you be my pacemaker."

The wonderful images, interesting contrasts, and the succinct descriptions of complex processes of healings, appeal to the counsellor in me. Such as: "The newsreel plays my life to me."

Then there are poems about God; no fluff or self righteousness; just love and reality "Call in anytime you're passing."

Just read it. You won't be disappointed.

                        Mary Cutts B.A. Grad.Dip. Couns.

Mary Cutts is a writer, poet and counsellor. She lectures in Trauma Recovery.

Her books include *God Image/Self Image* and *The Journey of Becoming*.

Other books by Chris Wren James

Beyond Prophetic : Hearing God's Voice
Naked I Stand: The Healing Journey
Naked I Stand: Workbook for Sexual Abuse Recovery

Email: christinefwren@hotmail.com
Website www.beprophetic.net
Fb ChristineWren James

Contents

Final Landing 1
Dermis 2
The Kiss 4
Chemistry 6
Tidal Wave 7
I, a Mere Man 9
Us 10
Pace Maker 11
Proposal 13
The Wall 15
Said the Words 18
The Counsellor 21
Skin 22
Love Landings 24
End the Beginning 26

Losing Sight 28
Eyes 29
The Lost Eye 32
My Friend, a Drowning Alcoholic 35

Place 36
Iona 37
Wood Cottage, Suffolk 39
Murwillumbah 41

Aftermath 44
Glass 45
No Trespassing 48
Betrayal 49

Sweat	51
Wise Woman	54
Your Heart	56
Poor	57
The Dark Side	59
The End of	60
Rescuer, Rescued	61
Naked, I Stand	63
Beyond You	64
To Give Again	66
Effexor: coming off anti-depressants after 3 years	68
As - Is	70
The Invisible Woman or: Becoming 60	71
Genetics	73
The Lost Voice	75
Trauma Recovery	77
Seeing Mary: Telling the Story	79
God	81
God	82
Undeserved Favour	84
The Campsite	86
Gratitude	87
Us. Older	88

Final Landing

Love has landed

Like an irreverent Cato

Leaping unexpected

Into my waiting arms.

The walls are down

And light thrusts the doors off their hinges

Making room for love's landing.

Your comfort-love heals every broken place

Waves flood salty with wholeness

This tide has knocked me sideways

I am limp

I am alive

But which way is up?

Dermis

I'm under your skin

Crawling about like the virus you caught in Madrid

Presenting me with a strong alternative.

You wont shed me quickly.

And I am here

In dilapidated fall-out

Running everywhere

Like a spilt keg of beer

Foaming at the edges.

Perhaps you could scrub me off

Like the dermis I've become?

An inoculation perhaps?

There's no storm now

The sun has shone upon me

And lights my way

Like a Suffolk Spring

But late in the coming, mind.

Dermis

I'm in your scales

Found wanting and wanton

An inescapable itch

You will always want to scratch.

Hopefully

The Kiss

No one's touched these lips for quite some time.

But your kiss yesterday

Evoked a wonder in me

Thought long dead.

Petal soft

Surprising joy

Deep care like salve.

The crash of my stone walls deafens me.

But far off

Miles below the ground

In the dragon's lair of memory

I hear the hungry want.

The monster

In its hibernating womb

Lifts a slow eyelid

Looks around,

The Kiss

And sniffs the draught of air coming down the chute.

Beast! You are supposed to be dead.
I killed you a long time ago-
Didn't I?

Chemistry

I can't quite see
If it's chemistry
Is it salt and light
Or day and night?
Opposites drawn
Crossed tides
Pulled like magnets
Taking sides.

And can I actually feel
In this middle age here
Those laid down moments
That now reappear?

I slither on the edge
Of a deepening pool
Am I in love
Or just an old fool?
But what's that swimming on the bottom?
I hope it's not carnivorous.

Tidal Wave

I am swept away by a tide
Not mine,
But God's.
And yours.

Light as the feathers I love
But heavy as myrrh
I am locked quite willingly in an embrace of three
Like the padlocks on the wires at Greenmount.
You surprise me God.
Your relentless pursuit
And intentionality rescues me.
Nothing random here.

And look now-
You've rocked my boat
My safe solo ride is over
You've tipped me out
To swim in waters

Tidal Wave

I've never known
But as I try for shore
To swim on
I feel your arms
Like Father's arms
That sweet familiarity
I'm here. I'm here.

I, a Mere Man

I'm out beyond the moon here
Out of my depth in the shallows
And I,
A mere man
Lost for words
In your verbosity
Am drowning in my sea.

And you,
Too intent on your prattle
To see my hand up,
Waving, attracting attention

As I sink.

Again.

Us

Kissed alive. Again.

Awakened forcibly

To feel. To enter in.

The slow dance begins.
Not quite tripping the light fantastic
Not even the Quick Step.
More one foot after the other.

Hear the faint door rap from the dungeon's gloom
Feed me.
The quiet beating of that scaly tail against the door
Might make me think again.

Pace Maker

Somewhere between minestrone and pav

I felt my heart change pace.
Your listening eyes drew me like a picture

In sound.

I've mapped my life 'til now

And clinked the door to possible.

Did I dream you?

Though when you know my secret --

And I shall hide it in my memory bank

Even if it bankrupts me—
Then we'll see.

Pace Maker

Clanging cymbals are not my style.

Rather I dare extend my borders

Let you through the ancient doors

Make room for you.

Pace myself.

Brace myself.

And let you be my pace maker.

Proposal

We lunched at Bella Kai, that day
Watched the heaving of a grey sea
And just before the Crème Brûlée
You said 'Marry me.'
You said 'I'll go down on bended knee
Right here
Right now.'
You said words to melt rock
Words that turned to diamonds and pearls
You said secrets never said
You melted me in a pool
Of gold, of tears
That scooped me up like saffron in sunlight
And hid me in your secret heart's compartment
Which I call home now.
It's a far pavilion
Away from the strife of tongues
And the prying eyes of those who know nothing

Proposal

And I-

Surprised by the joy of it all

Said simply : 'Yes. Yes please.'

The Wall

This wall, long guarded by vigilance

And these uniformed sentries,

Is finally down

Without fanfare or announcement.

I stand alone in the rubble

Each brick crafted and formed

Through fear and safe living.

Moulded and set with smug smiling precision

Now blitzed to a thousand pieces.

Exposed for all the world to see

The Wall

My heart on my sleeve

Dripping with anticipation

And pounding its beat

With precision.

The steady trail of possibilities

Winds up the hill

To my exploded rampart.

All the hopefuls,

Hearts in their mouths

Will she pick me?

The Wall

And I, wishing invisibility,

Crowd in on myself

Imploding release

But in terror of the plight of troth.

The vista widens

Dust forms

And I collect again

What is left

For masonry again.

Said the Words

So there it is. I've said it now.

It's out there.

Can't bring it back. And I'm glad in my sassy way.

Somehow, the winged bird

All healed and soaring now,

Not flapping at all,

Can come and go at will

Fly out

Land

Roost

Fly on.

I think those words are a homing pigeon

Coming home at last.

And my adolescent heart

Has delivered its decree

Made a declaration of its own

It's out there somewhere

Ricocheting off your walls

Said the Words

In its own unbelief
How bold. How brazen
Just couldn't wait.

But you are the one
Who crossed the floor
In one stride
Asked me to dance
Interlacing my fingers
As they all looked on
Curiously, wondering
About us.
'Well would you look at that!' they said.

And in my secret heart
Love welled up like a single tear
From my heart's eye
And burst from my mouth
In a gush of surprise
And in my secret heart

Said the Words

I hoped you'd think:
"God, she's beautiful"

Cinderella's prince.
I wonder if the shoe fits?
Perhaps too big after all.
And glass shoes make it hard to run.

The Counsellor

'So...'said the counsellor, eyes over glasses perched
on bony nose
Draconian eyes perusing my satisfied face

'Does he love you well?'
'Well enough' said I in smugness.
Thinking now, to love me well
Is to take the insurmountable
And add it to the sum of it all
And not blink an eye.

'Yes,' said I, 'Amazingly well. Considering.'

Skin

Our skin

Its soft animal hunger

Finding mine

There's a million hands of

Sensations unfolding

Like Champagne bubbles

Under the skin

Spreading celebration.

My skin's anorexic status

Is an embarrassment

To anybody interested.

I just want contact.

And soon

I've moved from where I was

To a foreign land

I don't know the rules here

Or even if there are any

I know what I want

Skin

But its off limits.

For the minute.

Love Landings

Love, like an aeroplane,

Is attempting to land.

There are no landing strips here.

But wait-

A light goes on – just faint, mind.

A waving hand

A feeble cry

Then a raw roar of beginning illuminates

And now

A neon blaze

Love Landings

Blinding as a sunburst.

The doors are off their hinges

In the rush for the runway.

But all that's heard

Is the distant drone
As the plane flies on.
Maybe next time.

End the Beginning

Lost ends are protruding like a half-finished basket
Being woven
Over and over
Same thread
Different basket
The weak spot always evident by its emphasis

You took cherries from my mouth
We fired our pips in competition
And laughed our heads off.
The sun kept on and on in that summer moment

Garden disclosures and half-said secrets
Spoken under the smell of honeysuckle

Moments of warm on stone walls
Lolling like labradors on a plaid rug

End the Beginning

We kept our hearts

Pure

 in a way.

Firmly

Under lock and key

In brand new metal trunks.

With padlocks. Fire resistant

We smouldered.

Burned even.

But never quite the spark

To carry the fire

Into the next field

Or the one after that.

And nothing happened

In one sense of the word.

Losing Sight

Eyes

These eyes have windowed width and depth

Been lost in space and air

A silent witness to far too much at times

And echoed back I see! I see!

Mirrored even you in their blue pools

Changing colour with moody winds

And gathered storms

Looked sideways catching glimpses and fragments

Of those who pilgrimmed past.

Closed in rapture

Eyes

Shut in terror

Flirted with life

Danced with death

Like shutters to the storm.

Don't look now….

These eyes remained unmoving in chaos and foolishness

Unblinking

Unblinkered

Washed over by one wave too many

Eyes

Across the shore of my face

Pooling as the tide goes out again.

Seeing is believing

But having believed, perceived.

I'm looking forward, me.

The Lost Eye

This poem was written 10 years before one of my sons actually did lose his eye.

And he,

Not knowing that the game was over

And nobody had won, really

And that

It's all fun and games til somebody loses an eye

And in fact

Somebody had lost an eye

And it's him.

The Lost Eye

And now there it was

All askew

And out of its socket

Dangling like so much bait on a hook

Never the same

And,

Despite cosmetic surgery

He knew.

He would always see the world

From a different perspective

The Lost Eye

And all the jokes about being one-eyed

Would pile up on the inside

Tumbling

Screaming and mocking

In the struggle to see the light, at least,

And walk a straight line.

A whole new meaning to being

Off your face.

My Friend, a Drowning Alcoholic

I think you have started to kill yourself

To take in poison like a sinking ship in the sea

It spreads to your edges and blunts them

I think you have started to wound what is the good in you

What is right

What has stood

The tests of time and tide

That wait for no man.

Slurred speech only falls on deaf ears

Blind eyes mean you cant see

And like dry rot,

Everything round you contaminates

The leaves fall off

Theres no more fruit

Just cactus in the dry dry land

That was your heart's red centre

Place

Iona

Waiting for the boat to cross

We saw Iona

Pink rock glinting in the pale sun

And soft seals, silent as leaf fall

Break in rings of water.

Wind wafts a shiver through the tall grass stems.

Stone crosses stamp the air.

Ancient as days.

And brings me from my mediocre into great space.

Abbey walls containing secrets

Held inside their cloistered halls

The feet of saints have trod this island

I feel their imprint on my soul.

Their feet have carried echoed words of life down through the ages

And Columba forged his link from Father's heart to earth, alight with holy flame.

Like the stable birth, all hidden from the probing eyes, except the few.

Iona

This little buried seed broke out, and, husk-free,
Sings and wings its way across the sea
Even as I lie in waving grasses, washed in salt air and silence
I am remembering and connected still.

Wood Cottage, Suffolk

Written in remembrance in Australia 2 months being back here.

I still miss that pheasant's cry
Those shrill plaintive notes
Signalling me
Cutting through a misty Suffolk morning
Like the herald of a new day
Miss the cherry-laden lane
Trees thick with crimson globs of sweet
Wheat waving under the great eye of sky
The flitting twitter of blue tits
Eave to willow and back and back
Their little feet
Trot stiletto in my roof.
I lie in bed and hear it all
But most of all the quiet stillness
No human voice to ruin reverie
The creak of ancient apple trunks against the shed

Wood Cottage, Suffolk

As spring sun warms

The chestnut blooms and little acorns

Peep from clustered leaves.

Promised life.

No cars passing. Heaven.

No jarring voices raised in protest

Silence in soliloquy

My place. My time.

Owls swoop through dusk light

Stars blink in wonder

A pale moon stares.

The cold air cuts my face as I breathe in damp

I think I am happy.

I am.

Murwillumbah

Approaching, at the 60 zone

Just at river bend

The dome comes down.

Not quickly, mind

But just encroachment level

Almost imperceptible

But there.

Soundless entrapment

No breath of moving air.

Its green beauty lulls my senses

Murwillumbah

Dark river currents

Cold terror waiting.

The significance of 'born and bred. Three generations, me.'

Or 'Whats not to love, eh?'

I'll give you a list as long as both my arms. Eh?

Throw my legs in as well.

I dream of seaweed shores and gull cry

The rush of waves and crab scuttle

Salt water, elixir of planets, of me.

Murwillumbah

Clear water moving, swooshing, alive and joyous

Not this stagnant dark secret sludge

In the here and the now.

My tunnel vision extends forever

Right at the end is a shaft of light-emitting-rays

Not sunshine

But hope.

The sea is my front water

Rushing to my shore to say

Yes. Yes and Yes.

Aftermath

Glass

Each glass shard cuts.
Some leave a scar
That hides behind something else
Altogether different.

You'd never know
There'd been an open heart
Cut with precision.

But sometimes

In your bland face

Looking outwards like a shop front

I catch a crossed section

Like a cracked window.

Glass

And the key turning in the lock

As the door closes.

And the shutters go down.

Again.

And you retire for the night.

But why wouldn't you?

And guard the treasure already ransacked

That left you shipwrecked

High and dry

Well just dry, really.

Glass

Looking for the shore again

A swimmer treading water
Arm raised
Hoping for rescue.

But this one will take a fleet of ships
Intent in their purpose
Carrying new glass windows
At least.

No Trespassing

So now the signs are up.

No entry. Wrong way. Go back.

It's a cul-de-sac. A dead end like a smoked cigar.

The barricades are thicker now

I'm peering through a glass darkly

Making sure we lock the gate

The dogs are tied

And the code set.

I hear gossip and the tsk of tongues

Tut-tutting what was us

Out of existence.

It's a hollow victory

But I hold my white flag high.

Not a winner to be found.

What do you mean- "Next time"?

There won't be one this side of the moon.

Betrayal

Your hidden agenda. Not mine.

What's mine? What's yours?

Going through the hidden drawers

Smooth as butter

Sharp as flint, you.

Somewhere at dawn light

You turned my heart to stone

Ran your sword through

 Neatly, mind.

While I was sleeping

You stole my heart and ran it through

Deftly skewered

Ashes in my mouth

My blood my bone

The acrid sulphur smell

Hanging in the air

A cloud between us

For good. Not my good, though.

Your velvet glove

Betrayal

Left no fingerprints

Threatened to silence

No proof except part of me left hanging on your hook.

Somewhere at dawn light

When I wasn't looking

My heart left.

Sweat

You left your clothes.

Heaped

Like so much muddle.

Clutter by the bed.

You let me pry and prise

You remained yourself.

For what its worth.

An unread letter

Your private self

Disengaged

Sweat

Out of bounds

What would it cost to prise those windows open?

The fee

Would bankrupt me

Your feline glance

Mocks my desire

You hold the cards

Call the tune

Keep the upper hand

And if I move too fast

Sweat

You'll vanish

And leave behind
Nothing

But your stale sweat

Like onions left too long.

Wise Woman.

Listen, Wise Woman.

Where were you in my dark night of my soul?

Where was your answer when I draped, helpless

From the lit lamp, moths buzzing about,

Pulling on my loose ends

To find a way out of the tangle?

Listen, Wolf.

Put those fangs away

My ripe white neck is not for you.

I fled the prairie long ago.

I'm out of reach.

Gone now.

Wisdom in hindsight

Is not what I need.

Get smart, wise woman

See the edge

As you approach.

Read the signs, idiot.

Wise Woman.

Wrong way. Go back.
You've burnt your bridges
So now what?

Your Heart.

Somewhere in a cavern

Under lock and key

Is a great trunk

Its locks and hinges rusty now

Dust and cobwebs cover.

Ropes secure the lid

And a black dog with bared teeth, on guard.

What treasure is such value here?

This is over kill.

A price beyond measure:

 your heart.

Guarded from a worse assault

Impoverished and fed with nothing much to speak of.

It feeds on the crumbs that fall between the crevices between us.

On occasion.

Poor.

Poor? Not really

Destitute perhaps, or

"Without visible means of support"

A collapsed building

Falling to oblivion

Where truth comes at last

In a forgotten land.

And truth is treasure.

Therefore I am rich

But never poor

Not talking "Calcutta"poor

Not "drunks under bridge"poor

Just an acknowledgement

A bereftness

Somehow lacking

Not quite all there

And certainly not by design or plan

But more the boat's gently nudging the shore

And coming home

Poor.

For the moment

Til the next launch.

The Dark Side.

Don't see the dark side

Where I hiss and spit

And weave the fabric with its weft and warp

Despairing of the interior garment where I live

At times, despising myself.

Just see the outer garment

Pretty sprigged flowers

Pulling you in

Like some Spring-searcher in a field.

My cover is just that: a cover.

It fits me well.

But sometimes leaks its dye

Into the cotton Springtime

Blooming on the outside.

Give me half a chance

I'd throw the whole coat to the Op shop

And start again.

But the pattern is in my skin , now.

The End of

There's a blunt knife edging through my flesh
As you are cut away from me.
More disapproval than acceptance.
There must be no proud flesh
No skin to skin.
We have filled with something like love
Stolen from jars high up on the back shelf
Unlabelled
Out of reach
"DANGER" all over them
We did not see the fine print
And cut our reaching hands on broken glass
As we licked the honey from our fingers.

Rescuer,

Rescued

'vulnerable' from Latin 'vulnerare' to wound:
1. capable of being wounded;

Rescuer, Rescued

2. Liable to injury
3. Open to a successful attack or damage

Naked, I Stand

Naked I stand

No longer ashamed

Covered by the wings that heal

My deep heart places.

Naked I stand

But hidden in the side of God

Open to some but not to all

I wander, but am not lost

Becoming vulnerable

Only to those that love

And hold me

Witth no questions asked

Well, 'No further questions.'

The "why" and "how"

Drop like stones to the bottom of the sea.

"I'm not quite sure" seems to cover

Most unknowns.

Beyond You

I am becoming myself

Keep completely still and you may find me

Layers off

Ripped by fire and wind

Skinned bone now

In my space not yours

Not theirs

Snatching pieces back like toys you stole

Words scramble for attention

Archived

Downwardly spiralling

Keeping still

My great discipline

Silence now mine

I see you

Rapping on my glass house

Marbled with friction and fracture

Safe from sound

Eyes closed

Beyond You

Blacking you out at last
I am beyond you.

To Give Again.

'You need to take a sabbatical' they said.

'Why?' said, I. 'I'm okay.'

'You're a fallow field', they said.

'So well sown

But so grimly reaped, now bare as a bone in a desert place.'

Its sticks and stones, like thrown names

Apparent on the surface

And dry, dry ground.

I see You, dear Father, bring a white cloth

Dripping plunged drops of myrrh and aloes

The quality of mercy

Waters sheets of blind compassion

Dripping through the holes in my skin

To bone, to soul

My ground soaks in

Wanting more, more

And when the ground is sodden with your type of love

To Give Again.

I hear you say:
'Give again. You're full.'
Are you mad, God ?

Effexor:
coming off anti-depressants after 3 years.

So I'm gone to ground

Plummeting down

From a clear blue sky

Startled to flight

But the flight down

is no flight at all.

But a mere drop.

In the ocean, no less.

Those little white grains

Have run my life for much too long

Measured out now

One by one

My wings are heavy as albatross

My forced day march

Exhausted

No puff left

Don't disturb me here

…or else.

Effexor: coming off anti-depressants after 3 years.

You've done your job
Dumbed me down
From manic bird
To sitting hen
What's it like to feel again?

As - Is

I am in 'as-is' condition

Like the garments at Vinnies.

Nothing in my pockets

Nothing up my sleeve

Agendas gone out with the garbage pick up

Deeply loved by ones that matter.

The rest don't count.

(Well only up to three.)

Empty cup waiting for filling

Choose your flavour

Pick your essence

Neutral gear for every thought

Choose the W for wise button

And abide no fools.

Sink or swim.

Your choice

The Invisible Woman or: Becoming 60

So. We're here again

Blanked out, blanked in and over

Like so much snow in a white out

Clawing at the glass here.

Anyone see me?

Unobserved, pecking at the seeds I'm thrown

A glassed chook

Hoping for more than a crumb

I stand

Devoured by passion to be, to do

To be able to happen to erupt to say to sing

Constraint my companion

And will the drums stop their rhythm

Noise enough to stop my thinking process?

Hiding in the sound

So I don't have to hear

Truth at my door knocking quietly

The Invisible Woman or: Becoming 60

Sorry, no one home today.
Call later when the chips are down
Or at least falling
Undisturbed

Light dawning now
Like those first obtrusive rays beneath my lid
curtain
It's what I most feared:
Not   quite   it.
The heart, vaulted chambers dank with shadow
Locked below the stone memorial
Never really seen the light of day
Barely beating
Needs a bit of air
I'm sending in the troops
Little flocks of birds in white formation
Pick pick pick
Come out! Come out!

Genetics

Roots bigger than branches, and running amok.

Genetics, the fault lines running and running

Stumbling over the bones of family connects

Falling for your mirrored self

And drowning in your own hallucination.

The synergy of pride and fall

Nothing at the top of the ladder

Just the white haze of disappointment

And lost dreams

Down the snake

Genetics

To start again. And again. And again.
Somewhere in your mind's eye
I became.
Am I the prototype
or just another clone
In man-made manufacture?
Whose fault line am I?
Can we lay the blame
Fairly and squarely
On old Grandma Hockings
And her upstart ways?
Is this my simple rebellion
That I wont sit in tidy rows
And listen to a boy of thirty two
Tell me how to live my life?

The Lost Voice.

Somewhere, in the night hours

You stole my voice

And rammed it on a spike

Up high on a shelf

Our of reach.

And you said 'You will never speak of this.'

"This", being the unspeakable

Turn of my life.

They said 'She's no trouble, really.

Always so quiet.

Sulks a bit, but hey-

Don't most kids?'

And I said nothing.

But a small rumble has shaken the top shelf

(Formerly out of reach)

And now I'm tall enough

And with help

I am a whisper

A sound

The Lost Voice.

A melody

A roar.

And I am bellowing

"This" was not okay.

Once, in a garden,

An angel came.

Handing me a gift

Wrapped in lavender silk

Was a pearl and a plume.

Her hand extended. She said

'Here. Sing with this. Write with this.'

And I do.

Trauma Recovery

I've listened to a thousand stories
Just like mine. Like yours.
I've heard you. Been there for you.
I've been the rescuer
Now it's my turn.
To tell it like it is.
Or was.
And now
Embodied in this safe cocoon
Soft wisps silk-woven
Keep me safe
From seen and unseen
Threads whisper
"This is who you are."
And I , unbidden
Merging from several into one,
The secret keepers
Speaking from your longest silence
Bring back the memory fragments
To make the life mosaic for the wall.

Trauma Recovery

From wings to centre stage.
Remember this? Remember that?
I do, now.
Was memory better left
In safety deposit boxes
Under the sea?

The ribbon unravels
The newsreel plays my life to me.
Where did I go when I wasn't looking?
There's archived history from the Torn Zone.

I thank the secret-keepers
Whose lips were sewn shut
Whose bodies took the stigma.

There's no flashing back or forward now.
Only a boat on a calm sea.

Heading for the next horizon.

Seeing Mary: Telling the Story

Each word, falling from its great height

Plummeting into its void of silence

Being heard, at last.

Stories never told, til now.

They echo down the waiting tunnel

Whose mouth devours each syllable

Like a train going to its destination.

Words hanging in the air

Like so many strings attached

To nothing.

Mary sits,

Compassion listening

Holds my hand

When the waters are deep.

'Stop. Breathe. Feel. Story. Attend.'

My mantra, now.

Gestalt – what a champion!

Speaking to an empty patch-worked chair

Raising my voice to a choir of hurrahs

Seeing Mary: Telling the Story

And quiet applause.

My heart, devoid of weight

Can fly now.

I'm off, over the rooftops

Looking down

Over the landscape

Escaping on the wind

With no turning back.

Except to say

'Thankyou, Mary.'

God

God

In God's heart

His infinite wisdom says

'Fall in here

Call in, anytime you're passing.

Unannounced.'

I'll find my falling mechanism

Learn to cut and release

And how to land

Unbidden

In the heart of all hearts.

God.

You take me as I am

No shame in that, at all.

You're a thousand shades of technicolour black and white

I love our life together

When I listen. And do.

You embrace me in my nonsense

And my rant.

God

I wake in your smile
Even when I'm blind.
When I need a good smack
You just look over your shoulder
And smiling broadly
With a little toss of the head
Say simply
'Come on.'

Undeserved Favour

Religion binds with ties of effort.

Subjugates.

My earning capacity of being undeserving

Eyes me squarely.

The hungry guard dog

Earning bones.

I can't deserve a love of undemand

I don't have it in me to return.

I'm in the dust of my own selfish ambition

Waiting to be counted on the planet

Undeserved Favour

Poor, naked, wretched and blind

Blinded to grace

Deafened to love-without-end

And your great bottomless pits of mercy.

How do I measure my value

Against the backdrop of all creation praising you, God?

But you say you notice a sparrow falling

How together is together?

Fragmentation is a fish shedding scales.

A flash of silver and it's gone

The Campsite

The lover of my soul

Has set up camp

In the smallness of me.

Fires blazing

He walks through the walls of my tent

Unbidden

An unexpected saviour laser-gazes his love through me.

He is extending tent pegs and lifting off the roof

Ignoring the No Trespassing signals I send.

My eye view is skewed

Irrevocably

I am seeing with my eyes wide open

Changed

Rearranged

And finally-

Me

Gratitude

I breathe my thanks

To air that holds

My breath

My cup is full

And overflows

It takes me in its river

To an ocean bright with hope

Sometimes in my blindness

I see an empty cup

A river bed of stone

And desert sand that

Fills my mouth with unbelief

You hold my eyes

But sighted

I drink deeply

And see my cup

Again in flow

Us. Older.

We won't see that springtime of our lives again

But in our old fashioned autumn tones

Devoid of techno aids (except for hearing)

Comes a simplicity

An understanding

A drawing of knowledge.

We share a smile with our Darjeeling

Pouring from a teapot with a cracked lid.

We watch the young ones fall in prepared holes,

Trying to let go and not to rescue

A set-up in so many ways.

We've fallen, you and I

Headlong sometimes

Arse-up

Sideways

But always getting up

To walk that extra mile

In each other's shoes.

Invisible to some

Us. Older.

But not each other

Just two silver hairs

Poddling our pilgrimage

Grateful for feet that walk. Albeit with bunions

And hearts that beat

In quiet cadence, even harmony.

Small conquests, but nothing to prove.

The everydayness of us

As comfortable as an old shoe

Is safe. Is reliable

I've done adventure, travelled the world

It over-rated itself

And cancelled itself out

Like a fraction on a page.

The accolades and triumphs fed me for a while.

But this? Now this, works.

This tried and tested time

Even with its broken sleep

Is a wonder to me.

And God, so cheeky and absurd

Us. Older.

Reminds me that He promised sap and vigour
In this autumn time we're in.

www.ingramcontent.com/pod-product-compliance
Lightning Source LLC
Chambersburg PA
CBHW051407290426

44108CB00015B/2184